International Labour Office

LABOUR DISPUTE RESOLUTION

An introductory guide

Robert Heron
and
Caroline Vandenabeele

ILO East Asia Multidisciplinary Advisory Team
ILO Regional Office for Asia and the Pacific
Bangkok

Copyright © International Labour Organization 1999

Publications of the International Labour Office enjoy copyright under Protocol 2 of the Universal Copyright Convention. Nevertheless, short excerpts from them may be reproduced without authorization, on condition that the source is indicated. For rights of reproduction or translation, application should be made to the ILO Publications Bureau (Rights and Permissions), International Labour Office, CH-1211 Geneva 22, Switzerland. The International Labour Office welcomes such applications.

Libraries, institutions and other users registered in the United Kingdom with the Copyright Licensing Agency, 90 Tottenham Court Road, London W1P9HE (Fax: +44 171 436 3986), in the United States with the Copyright Clearance Center, 222 Rosewood Drive, Danvers, MA 01923 (Fax: +1 508 750 4470), or in other countries with associated Reproduction Rights Organizations, may make photocopies in accordance with the licences issued to them for this purpose.

First published 1999

ISBN 92-2-111416-3

The designations employed in ILO publications, which are in conformity with United Nations practice, and the presentation of material therein do not imply the expression of any opinion whatsoever on the part of the International Labour Office concerning the legal status of any country, area or territory or of its authorities, or concerning the delimitation of its frontiers.

The responsibility for opinions expressed in signed articles, studies and other contributions rests solely with their authors, and publication does not constitute an endorsement by the International Labour Office of the opinions expressed in them.

Reference to names of firms and commercial products and processes does not imply their endorsement by the International Labour Office, and any failure to mention a particular firm, commercial product or process is not a sign of disapproval.

ILO publications can be obtained through major booksellers or ILO local offices in many countries, or direct from Customer Service, ILO Publications, International Labour Office, CH-1211 Geneva 22, Switzerland. A catalogue or list of new publications will be sent free of charge from the above address.

Printed in Thailand

Foreword

The promotion of sound labour relations and industrial harmony is generally accepted as a key element of national progress and development. But often labour conflicts or disputes, both individual and collective, override concern for harmony and cooperation, making them difficult goals to attain.

In such a scenario the effective resolution of labour disputes is a high priority. Of even greater importance is the need to prevent disputes of all types from arising in the first place.

This guide provides an overview of dispute prevention and resolution and stresses three basic principles. Dispute prevention through improved workplace cooperation comes first. Secondly, if dispute prevention proves impossible the parties should take steps to solve the problem themselves. Lastly, third party intervention should involve the disputing parties as much as possible.

The guide makes clear distinctions between negotiation and bargaining, conciliation, arbitration and adjudication in dispute resolution. It is intended as a resource for both group training and individual learning for employers, workers, representative organizations, and labour officials concerned with dispute prevention and settlement.

Related guides in the EASMAT series include: *Effective negotiation: A practical guide*; *Effective conciliation: A practical guide*; *Workplace cooperation: An introductory guide*; *Labour inspection policy and planning: A practical guide* and *Conducting labour inspection visits: A practical guide*.

As with other booklets in this series, its translation into national languages is encouraged. We would welcome comments and suggestions for improvement from users.

The guide has been prepared by Robert Heron, Senior Labour Administration Specialist, and Caroline Vandenabeele, Expert on Labour Law and Industrial Relations, of the ILO East Asia Multidisciplinary Advisory Team.

W.R. Simpson
Director
ILO East Asia Multidisciplinary
Advisory Team (ILO/EASMAT)

Bangkok
January 1999

Table of contents

Foreword	iii
1. Labour disputes: definitions	1
A. Labour disputes and industrial action	1
B. Types of labour disputes	3
2. Overview of dispute resolution	7
3. Labour inspection and dispute prevention	9
A. Enforcing the labour law	9
B. Informing and advising on the law	11
C. Problems not covered by the law	13
D. Power of inspectors	14
4. Collective bargaining and dispute resolution	15
A. Introduction	15
B. Collective bargaining and dispute prevention	17
C. Collective bargaining and dispute resolution	19
5. Dispute resolution within the enterprise	21

6. Conciliation and mediation	23
A. Definitions	23
B. Who can be a conciliator?	25
C. The conciliation process	27
D. Advantages of conciliation and mediation	28
E. Obstacles to conciliation	29
7. Arbitration	31
A. Definitions	31
B. Who can be an arbitrator?	32
C. The arbitration process	34
D. Advantages of arbitration	36
E. Obstacles to effective arbitration	37
8. Adjudication	39
A. General	39
B. Questions preliminary to the establishment of a specialized labour court	41

1 Labour disputes: definitions

A. Labour disputes and industrial action

A conflict is a disagreement between two or more parties. Where the disputing parties are labour and management, it is called an industrial conflict, a labour conflict or a trade conflict.

The disagreement may become apparent through **industrial action**. This is any form of action taken by one of the disputing parties to promote or protect its interests. Industrial action usually leads to disruption in production. The most common forms of industrial action are:

- **Ban**: a refusal by an individual worker or group of workers to undertake certain types of work, to use certain items of equipment or to work alongside other workers.

- **Go-slow**: a reduction in work effort or output, rather than a complete stoppage of work. This can be the result of a **work-to-rule** action where employees strictly follow all the rules and thus slow down the process.

- **Industrial sabotage**: damage by a worker or a group of workers to the employer's income by spoiling or disrupting the product or service offered, or damaging property or machinery used in the production process.

- **Lock-out**: the temporary closing down by the employer of a factory or establishment. During the lock-out, the workers are not entitled to any pay, since no work can be performed.

- **Strike**: a temporary stoppage or withdrawal from work by a group of workers. Strikers still consider themselves workers, with the right to return to their jobs once the dispute has been resolved. A strike can be supported by **picketing**. This involves workers on strike standing or walking in the surroundings of the workplace in order to inform other workers of the existence of a dispute or to persuade them not to enter the plant, as well as to prevent the employer from hiring new workers.

Industrial action can be:

- overt, such as a strike and picketing, or lock-out
- covert, such as sabotage
- organized
- unorganized
- individual
- collective.

Other, less formal, expressions of discontent include:

- increased labour turnover
- absenteeism
- tardiness.

An industrial conflict becomes a **dispute** when it is formalized in some way. This can include:

- industrial action
- a complaint by one of the parties
- one or both parties taking steps to resolve the conflict, e.g. through negotiation or seeking the intervention of a conciliator.

B: Types of labour disputes

Many national laws distinguish between different types of disputes. The two most commonly used classifications are:

- individual versus collective disputes
- rights versus interests disputes.

An **individual dispute** is a dispute between an individual employee and his or her employer.

A **collective dispute** involves a group of workers or their representatives and one or more employers. For a dispute involving a group of workers to be a real collective dispute, each member of that group must have the **same** grievance or claim. A collective dispute need not involve a trade union.

A **rights dispute** involves the interpretation or application of an **existing** right, as laid down in labour legislation, a collective agreement, an individual labour contract, or an existing practice. Rights disputes are commonly individual disputes.

> **Example:**
>
> A worker has a contract with his employer to be paid $120 per month. At the end of the month, the employer fails to pay the worker. The worker goes to a labour office to claim the wages due. This is a rights dispute because it concerns the right of a worker to receive $120 under his existing individual labour contract.

In some countries, with newly enacted labour legislation, workers and employers may be unaware of their rights and obligations under the law, leading to collective disputes concerning the application of existing rights.

An **interests dispute** involves a claim for **future** rights. Interests disputes usually result from a deadlock in collective bargaining. Most interests disputes are collective disputes.

> **Example:**
>
> During the renegotiation of a collective agreement, workers demand an increase in wages of 12%. Management offers an increase of 7%. The negotiations become deadlocked and the workers go on strike. This is an interests dispute, since it concerns the desire of workers for terms or benefits that they currently do not enjoy.

Some Asian countries speak about **trade disputes**, which usually comprise **all** disputes between workers and employers, regardless of whether they are individual or collective disputes, rights or interests disputes.

> **Example**:
>
> Section 2 of the Malaysian Industrial Relations Act of 1967 defines a trade dispute as "any dispute between an employer and his workmen which is connected with the employment or non-employment or the terms of employment or the conditions of work of any such workmen".

A further classification is sometimes made for:

- disputes over unfair labour practices, and

- recognition disputes

Disputes over unfair labour practices arise from attempts by the management of an enterprise to discriminate against workers for being trade union members or for participating in trade union activities.

Recognition disputes arise when the management of an enterprise or an employers' organization refuses to recognize a trade union for the purpose of collective bargaining.

In most national legislations, the **resolution procedure** depends on the type of dispute. In most cases, the procedure depends on whether the dispute is a rights or an interests dispute, but may also provide for different arrangements for recognition disputes or disputes over unfair labour practices. Some countries apply a different procedure solely depending on whether the dispute is individual or collective. But as the majority of individual disputes are rights disputes and the majority of collective disputes are interests disputes, this is not a major difference in practice.

2 Overview of dispute resolution

- The term **dispute resolution** is sometimes used to describe all ways of ending a dispute.

- But when an explicit distinction is made between **dispute resolution** and **dispute settlement,** resolution usually refers to resolving disputes through negotiation, conciliation and mediation in which the disputing parties take prime responsibility for solving their problems. Settlement refers to arbitration and adjudication in which a third party imposes a decision to finally settle the dispute.

- There are three sequential principles in dispute resolution:

    ♦ Prevention is better than resolution.

    ♦ If prevention is impossible, the disputing parties should resolve the problem themselves.

    ♦ If the disputing parties cannot resolve their problem, any third party intervention should involve the disputing parties as much as possible.

Dispute prevention can be achieved through:

- effective workplace cooperation (see: *Workplace cooperation: An introductory guide, ILO/EASMAT*);

- effective labour inspection (see: *Conducting labour inspection visits: A practical guide* and *Labour inspection policy and planning: A practical guide, ILO/EASMAT*);

- distributing information on workers' and employers' rights and obligations. This can be achieved through:

    - formal education and training programmes held, for example, in enterprises, in senior schools and vocational training institutions

- the mass-media, such as radio and television spots or a weekly labour column in newspapers

- distribution of leaflets and brochures.

Dispute resolution by the parties themselves will be done mainly through negotiations and collective bargaining. Once an agreement has been reached, it can prevent further disputes (see Chapter 4: "Collective bargaining and dispute resolution"; see also: *Effective negotiation: a practical guide, ILO/EASMAT*).

Dispute resolution through the intervention of a third party, includes:

- informal contacts initiated by the disputing parties, with an intermediary, within the enterprise

- conciliation and mediation

- arbitration

- adjudication.

> **Dispute prevention is far better than dispute resolution.**

3 Labour inspection and dispute prevention

Labour inspectors have an important role to play in dispute prevention, particularly in individual rights disputes.

Labour inpectors:

- enforce labour laws and related regulations

- advise employers and workers on how to comply with the law

- report to their supervisors on problems and defects not covered by law.

A. Enforcing the labour law

Labour inspectors can prevent labour disputes by enforcing laws concerning:

- the terms and conditions of work, including wages, hours, leave and overtime payment

- workplace safety and health.

These matters are a potential source of conflict between workers and employers and can lead to industrial disputes if not addressed quickly and fairly.

Routine labour inspection visits in which inspectors check compliance with the law can prevent problems from escalating into disputes. Such visits are normally unannounced - the inspector visits the enterprise without appointment.

Example

Labour regulations determine that the minimum wage payable to workers is $40 per month. During an inspection visit the inspector finds that the employer pays $30 per month. There is potential conflict between workers and the employer but the problem is resolved by the inspector enforcing the law - ordering the employer to pay $40 plus any arrears.

B. Informing and advising on the law

Labour inspectors are required to do more than simply enforce the law. They are required to inform and advise employers **and** workers by:

- explaining what the law says
- indicating where legal requirements are not met
- explaining what needs to be done to comply with the law.

By advising on how to comply with the law inspectors can prevent problems from arising.

In explaining the meaning of the law, inspectors must be:

- accurate
- up-to-date
- impartial

When giving advice, inspectors should concentrate on what needs to be done, rather than on the technical details of how to do it.

Example:

During an inspection visit workers complain about excessive dust levels. This represents a source of potential conflict between workers and management.

The inspector detects that the dust level, in fact, is higher than the law allows and advises the employer to install an exhaust system. By so doing, the inspector has advised the employer **what must be done** to comply with the law concerning dust levels and prevented a conflict which may have led to a dispute.

But it is not the inspector's task to design the exhaust system and supervise its installation.

Example:
During an inspection visit the employer indicates that if he continues to pay the minimum wage required by law he will not make a profit, his business will close and all workers will lose their jobs.

The inspector advises that in certain circumstances the enterprise can apply for an exemption from minimum wage provisions. The inspector explains how it may be possible to pay less than the minimum but still comply with the law.

But it is not the inspector's task to make the application for the exemption on the employer's behalf.

In advising on how to comply with the law, inspectors have to take decisions based on their knowledge and experience.

Example:

How much time should the inspector allow the employer to install an exhaust system to eliminate the dust problem?

If the time is too long the risk of conflict increases. If the time is too short, the employer will not be able to comply.

Example:

How much time should the inspector allow the employer to make back-payments where wages have been underpaid?

If the time is too long workers are denied their legal rights and the risk of conflict leading to a dispute increases. If the time is too short, the employer will not be able to obtain the necessary funds.

C. Problems not covered by the law

While conducting inspection visits, inspectors may find problems not covered by the law. Such problems can be a source of conflict and can lead to a labour dispute.

In these cases, the inspector should:

- identify the problem
- describe it in writing
- report it to his/her superiors.

Defects and problems reported in this way can be used as a basis for amending the law and thus preventing disputes in the future. But until the law is amended, the inspector will have to rely on other approaches to resolving conflict such as, for example, encouraging consultation, discussion and negotiation.

Example:

While conducting an inspection visit, the inspector learns that the workers are planning some form of industrial action because they have learned that a fellow worker is HIV positive. The workers consider this to be a risk to their health and insist that the affected worker should be dismissed. The employer argues that the HIV worker is performing his duties, that he does not pose a risk to other workers' health, and there are no grounds for dismissal.

The inspector knows of no laws or regulations covering this problem and reports it to his superiors. In time, the law may be amended and future problems of this type can be solved by the inspector enforcing the law. But for now, the inspector should aim to prevent a dispute by providing accurate and up-to-date information about HIV and the ways in which it can and cannot be transmitted – and then encouraging the parties to find a mutually acceptable solution.

D. Power of inspectors

Preventing disputes requires that inspectors use various powers available to them. This includes power to:

- freely enter workplaces liable to inspection
- enter workplaces without appointment
- carry out examinations or tests to determine whether the law is being observed
- interview workers and employers
- examine books and documents concerning working conditions
- issue orders requiring alterations to plant or installation
- issue orders with immediate effect if there is imminent danger to workers' safety and health
- initiate legal proceedings against the employer.

In addition to these powers conferred by law, labour inspectors can draw on their knowledge, skills and accumulated experience, as well as their ability to relate to and interact with other people, to help them to resolve conflict and prevent labour disputes.

4 Collective bargaining and dispute resolution

A. Introduction

Collective bargaining is a process of voluntary negotiation between an employer or group of employers and a workers' organization or group of workers with a view to reaching mutually acceptable terms and conditions of employment.

The process is based on **negotiation** which assumes:

- a **conflicting interest** which creates the need to negotiate

- a **common interest** which provides the motivation to reach agreement.

The collective bargaining process requires that:

- the parties are **free** to associate

- the employer or group of employers **recognizes** a group of workers for bargaining purposes

- the parties are **committed** to make the process work

- the parties have the **ability** to bargain

- the legal and political **environment** is supportive of the bargaining process.

The **general purpose** of collective bargaining is to establish rules covering the employment relationship. These rules can be:

- substantive

- procedural

Substantive rules refer to the actual terms and conditions of employment including wages, allowances, hours of work, leave and work safety.

Procedural rules refer to the process and arrangements to be followed in establishing the substantive rules and for resolving disagreements and disputes.

The specific purposes of collective bargaining are to:

- set wages and conditions of employment
- regulate labour-management relations
- complement the minimum standards established by legislation
- prevent labour disputes
- resolve labour disputes.

B. Collective bargaining and dispute prevention

Collective bargaining prevents disputes by sharing power in the workplace.

Potential conflicts over the terms and conditions of employment are avoided by ensuring that workers are:

- informed
- consulted
- involved in making binding decisions which affect them.

Wages and other monetary benefits are determined by discussion and mutual agreement.

Disagreements are aired at the bargaining table and compromises reached.

Example

Workers demand an increase in wages of $20 per month. The employer offers $5. There is a disagreement and potential grounds for a dispute.
But through a process of gradual convergence the parties reach a mutually acceptable figure. The workers might reduce their demand to $16 and the employer might increase his offer to $8. This process continues until an agreement is reached at, say, $11. The willingness of the parties to continue to talk and to reach a compromise prevents their conflict from becoming a labour dispute.

Disputes will be prevented by devoting time in the bargaining process to discussion - which involves talking, listening, asking questions and generally sharing information and ideas.

This will help to:

- clarify meanings
- eliminate misunderstandings
- express intentions in clear and simple terms.

A key factor in further preventing disputes through collective bargaining is to ensure that what is agreed by the parties is:

- clear
- unambiguous
- not open to misinterpretation

Example:

A collective agreement which states "workers are entitled to 14 days paid annual leave" is not clear and could lead to a dispute. The agreement should clearly specify who is a worker, which workers are so entitled and whether the 14 days refer to working days or to calendar days.

C. Collective bargaining and dispute resolution

The process of collective bargaining enables the parties to resolve disputes which arise under their agreement.

It is the parties' agreement and it is in their interests to resolve disputes by themselves rather than rely on the intervention of a third party.

Disputes can arise concerning:

▸ the interpretation of **existing** provisions under the agreement

Example:

Under a collective agreement workers are entitled to paid leave on religious festival days. Which workers? What is a religious festival day? Which religions?

Example:

Under a collective agreement, workers are entitled to one extra day's annual leave for each year of service. What is the position of a worker with one year and 11 months of service? Is he or she entitled to one or two extra days? If this results in a dispute between the parties, it could be resolved by discussion and negotiation to reach agreement on whether "each year of service" means each full-year, or each part-year. If the parties cannot agree, they would then follow the dispute procedures as outlined in their collective agreement.

Disputes over issues such as those outlined in the above examples could have been prevented by more careful drafting of the collective agreement.

- disputes can also arise concerning the negotiation of **new** provisions once the existing agreement expires.

Example:

In negotiating a new collective agreement, workers demand a wage increase of 20% based on increases in the cost of living and increased labour productivity. The employer offers 6% based on capacity to pay.

Negotiations become deadlocked with neither party prepared to change its position. A labour dispute is declared and the workers take industrial action.

Collective agreements will normally include a set of procedures to resolve disputes, involving the following steps:

- bargaining between the two parties to break the deadlock

- if bargaining fails to resolve the dispute, an independent third party is appointed to conciliate or mediate. The conciliator may be a private person or a government official, depending on what the parties have agreed. Conciliation is an extension of the bargaining process with the conciliator assisting the parties to reach an agreement.

- if conciliation fails, the parties will have to revert to bargaining or, alternatively, have the dispute settled by arbitration. The arbitrator will be appointed in accordance with the provisions of the collective agreement. The arbitrator has the power to make a decision that is binding on both parties.

5 Dispute resolution within the enterprise

Dispute resolution within the enterprise:

- involves discussions between worker(s) or their representative(s) and management or its representative(s);

- usually follows a number of sequential steps laid down in an agreed procedure, which may be part of a collective agreement or code of conduct;

- may progressively involve higher levels of management and workers' representatives;

- may include negotiation and collective bargaining.

> **Dispute resolution within the enterprise is a preferred means of settling disputes, since it encourages the parties themselves to take responsibility for resolving their problems.**

Dispute resolution within the enterprise can be done through a respected and trusted person within the enterprise accepted by both parties as a suitable intermediary. In some countries this person is referred to as an ombudsperson. The tasks of this person may involve:

- hearing and informally investigating complaints and grievances
- encouraging open communication
- facilitating and guiding the problem-solving process
- providing additional information
- advising both parties on approaches to conflict management.

Although this third party is usually designated by management, he or she must have the full approval of the workers in the enterprise and be seen as someone who can be trusted.

The intermediary must maintain strict confidentiality concerning the names of the parties and the issue in dispute. In some cases, however, the party making the complaint may give permission for his or her name to be disclosed.

> **Example:**
>
> A group of workers are having difficulties with their supervisor, who is treating them in an aggressive and impolite way. The enterprise has an intermediary (ombudsperson). One of the workers visits the intermediary to complain about the supervisor and to try to find a solution to this problem. The intermediary will talk to the supervisor and tell him that the workers have difficulties with his behaviour.
> The intermediary will not indicate to the supervisor the name of the complaining worker, unless that worker gives approval.

In addition to maintaining confidentiality, the intermediary must act impartially, irrespective of his/her position in the enterprise.

6 Conciliation and mediation

A. Definitions

Conciliation is a form of dispute resolution in which a third, neutral party, the conciliator, assists the parties in reaching an agreement or finding an amicable solution.

Conciliation in the strict sense of the word, differs from **mediation** insofar as:

- the conciliator acts as a facilitator, bringing people together, actively taking part in the resolution process but without proposing solutions;
- a mediator is more actively involved and suggests proposals and methods for actually resolving the dispute.

The difference between a conciliator and a mediator is often academic. A good conciliator or mediator will make various suggestions or proposals to solve a problem and break a dead-lock; he/she, however, will never impose a solution: it is still up to the parties to reach agreement.

Conciliation differs from **arbitration** in that an arbitrator considers the arguments of both sides and then takes a decision that is binding on the parties in the dispute.

A distinction can be made between **voluntary conciliation** and **obligatory conciliation**.

- In some countries, the law allows disputing parties to decide whether they want to submit their dispute to conciliation or not.

  The reasoning behind **voluntary conciliation** is that there is no point in trying to conciliate if the parties are not convinced that this is an appropriate way to resolve their dispute.

- In other countries, conciliation is **compulsory**. This does **not** mean that the conciliation process **must** result in an agreement; it simply means that some steps of the process are compulsory, such as the obligation to attend a conciliation meeting when invited.

  The reasoning behind compulsory conciliation is that the parties need to be educated about the advantages of a cooperative, rather than conflictual, approach to dispute resolution.

> **Conciliation is bargaining with the assistance of an independent, neutral third party.**

B. Who can be a conciliator?

Conciliation services can be provided by:

- private persons
- government.

Conciliation is essentially a one-person job. Individual conciliators can do the job:

- on a full-time basis
- on a part-time basis, which is mostly the case for labour officers, who may have other responsibilities
- on an ad hoc basis, which may be the case for private conciliators.

In some countries, conciliation takes place through **conciliation boards or committees.** These bodies can be established:

- at enterprise level
- at local or provincial government level
- at national level.

Conciliation boards may appoint individual conciliators to the work, in which case the main task of the Board is deciding whom to appoint.

Conciliation boards or committees can be set up on a permanent or ad hoc basis.

- If on a **permanent** basis and it is a tripartite body, employers' and workers' organizations will nominate or select their representatives to sit with government appointed members.

- If on an **ad hoc basis**, the conciliation board or committee will be established when a dispute arises. If the body is tripartite, the workers and employer(s) involved will each usually nominate a member to the board.

- The permanent and ad hoc approaches may be combined, so that there is a list of potential panel members from which the parties to a dispute can select the members of the conciliation body that will handle their dispute

A conciliator does **not** need any **formal qualifications**, such as being a lawyer, an economist, a psychologist, or an accountant. The conciliator needs a good knowledge of:

- the national economy in general
- the national industrial relations system
- the applicable laws and regulations
- the social actors
- the particular industry.

At a **personal level**, the conciliator needs to be:

- committed to his/her job
- impartial and independent
- patient
- sincere
- a good listener and communicator.

C. The conciliation process

The conciliation process has three major steps – preparing for the conciliation, conducting the conciliation, and the outcomes and follow-up.

In **preparing** for a specific conciliation, the conciliator will:

- make initial contact with the disputing parties
- collect and analyse background information
- decide how to guide the conciliation
- design a conciliation plan.

In **conducting** the conciliation, the conciliator will:

- open the conciliation
- define the issues and agree on the agenda with the parties
- interact with the parties
- come up with options for settlement
- assist the parties in their final bargaining, but without imposing a solution.

Once the conciliation is **finished**, the conciliator has to:

- draft the agreement
- make a conciliation report
- do some follow-up if no agreement between the parties is reached, such as a fact-finding procedure.

Each of these specific steps is explained in detail in: *Effective conciliation: A practical guide,* ILO/EASMAT.

D. Advantages of conciliation and mediation

Conciliation and mediation are often applied to interests disputes, where there is no clear-cut answer to a problem. The advantages of conciliation and mediation are:

- the parties remain in control of the outcome of the process

- it is a flexible process

- it is a private process

- it is a peace-making process

- it avoids the uncertainties of a judicial or arbitral decision

- it leaves room for an innovative, imaginative resolution of a dispute

- it can safeguard the ongoing relationship between the parties, since it is less conflictual than, for example, arbitration.

E. Obstacles to conciliation

Conciliation is not easy. There are several possible obstacles which may make it difficult for the conciliator to assist the parties to find an amicable solution to their dispute. These include:

- the conciliator is seen as being biased
- the conciliator does not prepare well enough for the case
- the conciliator has a possible solution to the dispute in mind, and imposes this on the parties
- one or both disputing parties does not really want to conciliate and accepts an agreement which it later does not carry through
- the conciliator has a heavy workload and therefore forces an agreement upon the parties
- one of the disputing parties is much stronger than the other and dominates proceedings
- one or both parties are represented by lawyers who concentrate on legal argument rather than the real issues.

7 Arbitration

A. Definitions

Arbitration is a form of dispute settlement in which an independent third party considers the arguments of both sides and then takes a decision binding on the parties to the dispute.

Adjudication, or the settlement of a dispute through a court, is also a form of arbitration in that there is a neutral third party who takes a binding decision. Differences between arbitration and adjudication relate to:

- **enforcement of the decision.** If one of the parties does not follow the arbitration award, the other party will have to go to court to have the decision enforced.

- **appeal.** Although the decision taken by an arbitrator is binding, an appeal may be possible. This appeal will have to be handled through adjudication.

- In some countries, adjudication is directed to rights disputes, while arbitration in the strict sense of the word, is concerned with interests disputes.

Arbitration can be compulsory, obligatory or voluntary.

- **Compulsory arbitration** is arbitration required by law.

- **Obligatory arbitration** results from the voluntary agreement of parties under a collective agreement to submit future disputes related to that agreement to an arbitrator for settlement.

- **Voluntary arbitration** is a mutual request by labour and management after a dispute has arisen, that an issue on which they do not agree be submitted to an arbitrator for settlement.

B. Who can be an arbitrator?

Arbitration services can be provided through:

- private arrangements in which both parties agree on a person to take a decision concerning their dispute
- by the government.

Arbitration can be done through:

- a single arbitrator
- an arbitration board.

The advantage of a **single arbitrator** considering the case, is that it is less time-consuming than when a board has to decide on a dispute. This is so for both the hearing itself and the process of reaching a decision.

Arbitration boards can be:

- tripartite, including a neutral independent arbitrator as well as members appointed by workers' and employers' organizations
- fully neutral and independent in composition.

The advantages of a **tripartite arbitration board** include the presence of workers' and employers' representatives as members making it easier to appreciate the general background of the conflict.

The advantages of **a neutral board** include that it may have several experts (e.g. a lawyer, an economist, a financial expert) who can provide an in-depth analysis of problems from their technical perspectives.

Arbitration bodies can be:

- ad hoc, which may be the case for voluntary arbitration
- permanent, which is likely to be the case for obligatory and compulsory arbitration.

An arbitrator does **not** need any **formal qualifications**, such as being a lawyer or an economist. The arbitrator needs a good knowledge of:

- the economy in general
- the national industrial relations system
- the applicable laws and regulations, including the procedures to be followed in an arbitration hearing
- workers' and employers' organizations
- the particular industry in which the dispute has arisen.

On a personal level, the arbitrator needs to:

- be impartial
- have good analytical skills
- be patient
- possess good drafting skills.

C. The arbitration process

The arbitration process has three major steps - preparing for arbitration, conducting arbitration, and writing the arbitration award.

In **preparing** for arbitration, the arbitrator will:

- contact the parties to inform them about the arbitration process, and the time and place of the hearing. The arbitrator should not discuss the case with any of the parties

- summon witnesses and experts where necessary.

In conducting arbitration, the emphasis is on the **hearings**. During the hearing:

- the arbitrator will open the proceedings

- each of the parties will present its case

- the arbitrator may ask questions to seek clarification

- witnesses and experts may be invited to clarify certain issues

- on-site visits may be possible.

After the hearing, the arbitrator will have to write an **arbitration award,** embodying his or her decision. The decision will have to be carefully written to avoid ambiguities and to prevent new problems from arising from the interpretation of the award. Depending on national legislation and practice, the award can:

- simply set out the decision taken by the arbitrator, or

- set out the decision as well as the reasons for that decision.

Arbitration awards are binding on both parties. If, however, one of the parties refuses to execute one of the provisions of the award, the other party will have to apply to a court to have the decision enforced. Legislation may also provide that the decision of an arbitrator can be appealed against to a court, on various legal grounds. In such a situation, it will be helpful if the court has available to it a clear, well-reasoned decision in the form of the arbitration award.

D. Advantages of arbitration

The advantages of arbitration include the following:

- It may be less time-consuming than bargaining, conciliation and mediation.

- It can end a deadlock between the parties.

- In some cases, the parties choose the arbitrator, thereby giving them a feeling of "ownership" of the dispute and a commitment to its outcome.

- It requires the parties to prepare for a hearing in which their arguments will be subjected to independent scrutiny. This may encourage them to focus on key issues.

- The hearing does not follow formal court-room procedures, creating a less confrontational approach to the problem.

E. Obstacles to good arbitration

The obstacles to effective arbitration include the following:

- The arbitrator may be perceived as biased by the parties. The arbitrator may "advocate" instead of arbitrate.

- The hearing may become dominated by the legal arguments of legal counsels at the expense of the substantive issues.

- The hearing may take longer than expected, due to the delaying tactics of one or both parties.

- The decision may not be acceptable to either party, thereby raising the possibility of further conflict and disputation.

- The arbitrator's award may be ambiguous and confusing.

8 Adjudication

A. General

Adjudication is the settlement of a dispute through a court. Adjudication is often used:

- to settle individual rights disputes
- as a form of appeal against a decision made by an arbitrator
- as a last resort, if all other means of dispute resolution have failed.

In adjudication, an independent, neutral, third party – a judge – takes a decision which is binding on the parties.

A question often raised in relation to labour adjudication is whether there is a need for specialized courts, or whether labour disputes can and should be settled through civil courts. It has been argued that a labour contract is no different from any other form of contract and that disputes over labour issues can thus be settled through civil courts.

There are, however, a number of characteristics which distinguish labour cases from civil cases, and support the need for separate labour courts.

(1) The distinct nature of the conflict

- A labour contract is not a one-off contract. In many cases, workers and employers may have to continue to work together long after the dispute has been settled.
- Decisions in labour disputes can have far-reaching consequences for the individual, family and social life of workers in particular.

▸ The role of the judge thus becomes one of promoter of social justice and peace in addition to the role of adjudicator.

(2) The different composition of a labour court

Considering the special nature of labour conflicts, there is a need to seek solutions which are acceptable to all parties.

This will be best achieved if the parties are involved in the decision-making process, for example, through courts established on a tripartite basis, comprising representatives from government, workers' and employers' organizations.

(3) The different procedure involved

Given the different nature of labour conflicts, and in particular the ongoing day-to-day relationship between workers and employers, there is a need for **quicker, less expensive and less formal** procedures than the civil court jurisdiction can provide.

This will be best achieved through separate specialized courts, having separate procedural rules and presided over by judges who have knowledge and experience of labour issues.

B. Questions preliminary to the establishment of a specialized labour court

When establishing a separate labour court, there are many issues that need to be considered. The most relevant are set out below.

- **How many judges** will sit in the court?

    There are several options including;

    (a) one or more professional judge(s), specializing in labour law

    (b) a tripartite court with one professional judge and two lay judges.

- Questions related to **lay judges**

    (a) On what basis will lay judges be selected?

    If the lay judges are appointed by their respective workers' and employers' organizations, it should be clear that under no circumstances can they receive instructions from their organizations. Nor should these organizations be allowed to withdraw the appointment of their representatives.

    The objectivity of lay judges must be guaranteed. A possible measure, therefore, is to guarantee the anonymity of the vote of the judges.

    (b) In a tripartite labour court, will lay judges have the same decision-making power as the professional judge, or is their role solely advisory?

- Who can **summon** a party to appear before the court? In the case of workers, is it the individual, or can a worker only summon through his/her union?

- What are the possibilities for **appeal**? Is an appeal possible in any case or only on questions of law, but not on questions of fact?

- What is the interrelationship between conciliation, arbitration and the labour court?

    (a) Are arbitration and conciliation institutions part of the court system or are they totally separate institutions?

    (b) Can an appeal be made to a labour court after a dispute is handled through arbitration?

    (c) Is there an obligation for the labour judge to try and conciliate the dispute prior to adjudication?

- Should there be one or several **divisions** in the labour court, each dealing with specific questions?

- Can the parties be **represented** in court or not? Do they need to be represented? Who can represent them (e.g. can a worker be represented by a union and an employer by an employers' organization?) Are lawyers allowed to represent the parties? In case of representation, do the parties still have to appear in person at the hearing?

- What will be the **scope of jurisdiction of the court?**

    (a) Will it have jurisdiction over collective and/or individual disputes?

    (b) Will it have all-inclusive or partial jurisdiction in labour matters?

Example:

A worker is dismissed for alleged theft. Can the labour court hear the whole case and decide whether or not there is enough evidence that the worker stole goods from the employer and that the dismissal therefore was justified? This is all-inclusive jurisdiction. Or is it the criminal court that will decide whether the worker is guilty or not of theft with its decision being binding on the labour court? This is partial jurisdiction.

(c) Will its jurisdiction be exclusive or concurrent with that of other courts? Can a civil court also hear labour cases, or can this only be done by the labour court?

www.ingramcontent.com/pod-product-compliance
Ingram Content Group UK Ltd.
Pitfield, Milton Keynes, MK11 3LW, UK
UKHW041956230426
12048UKWH00008B/378